MAY   2012

FIRE DISASTER

Chris Oxlade

ARCTURUS

This edition first published in 2011 by Arcturus Publishing

Distributed by Black Rabbit Books
P.O. Box 3263
Mankato
Minnesota MN 56002

Printed in China

Library of Congress Cataloging-in-Publication Data

Oxlade, Chris.
 Fire disaster / Chris Oxlade.
    p. cm. -- (Emergency!)
 Includes index.
 ISBN 978-1-84837-953-4 (library binding)
 1. Fires--History--Juvenile literature. I. Title.
 TH9448.O95 2012
 363.37--dc22

                            2011006642

Series concept: Alex Woolf
Editor and picture researcher: Alex Woolf
Designer: Ian Winton

Picture credits
Corbis: cover (Chris Cheadle/All Canada Photos), 7 (RubberBall), 8 (Bettmann), 9 (Bettmann), 10 (Bettmann),
11, 12 (Bettmann), 13 (Bettmann), 15 (Bettmann), 17 (Jonathan Blair), 18 (Bettmann), 19 (Jonathan Blair),
22 (Reuters Television), 23 (Menno Boermans/Sygma), 26 (Andrew Brownbill/epa), 27 (HO/Reuters), 28 (Phil
McCarten/Reuters), 29 (Juice Images).
Rex Features: 20 (Sipa Press), 21 (Sipa Press), 24, 25 (Mike Jones).
Shutterstock: 4 (Arcady), 5 (Darin Echelberger), 6 (Kazela), 16 (Jan Erasmus).

Cover picture: Firefighters tackle a house fire in British Columbia, Canada.

Every attempt has been made to clear copyright. Should there be any inadvertent omission, please apply to the
publisher for rectification.

Supplier 03, Date 0411, Print Run 1048
SL001697US

Contents

Fire!

Lights flash, sirens wail, and smoke billows. Firefighters grapple with heavy equipment. Jets of water from hoses disappear into leaping flames. Ambulances wait for the injured. Police hold back the crowds and traffic. These are all familiar sights from the scene of a fire disaster.

What is fire?

Fire is one of the most frightening foes for the emergency services. It is a terrible destructive force. In order to fight it, firefighters must first understand what it is. So what exactly is fire? In essence, fire is a chemical reaction that happens when a substance combines with oxygen from air. The reaction makes heat, light, and smoke.

This is the fire triangle. It shows that oxygen, heat, and fuel are needed for a fire. Firefighters remove one of these elements to put out a fire.

OXYGEN

HEAT

FUEL

Effects and causes

Fire destroys materials such as wood and rubber, melts plastics, bends and twists metals, and causes explosions. Fire is harmful to people, causing burns on skin. And smoke chokes people, stopping them from breathing.

A terrifying house fire like this can be started by a small accident such as a candle being knocked over.

There are many ways for a fire to start. It can be caused by discarded matches and cigarettes, out-of-control campfires, electrical faults, explosions, accidents with naked flames such as candles, stoves, lightning, and even meteorites.

AT-A-GLANCE

Fire losses, USA, 2009
- 3,010 deaths
- 17,050 injuries
- approx $12.5 billion damage

5

Firefighting

Emergency telephone calls from the public are routed to an emergency control center. The controller who answers the call passes a message to the fire service, the police or the ambulance service. When somebody reports a big fire, all three emergency services respond.

At the scene

At the fire station nearest to the scene of the fire, firefighters jump into their fire trucks, ready for action. Arriving at the fire, the leading firefighter makes a plan to tackle it. He or she might call for extra help if the blaze is too big.

It might take dozens of firefighters to deal with a major blaze like this.

Fire triangle

Firefighters know all about the fire triangle (see page 4). They put out flames by removing one side of the triangle (heat, fuel or oxygen). For example, pouring water on a fire cools it down, so it removes the heat. And spraying foam on a fire stops oxygen getting to the fuel.

Firefighters go into burning buildings to rescue people who are trapped by the flames.

SAVING LIVES

One of the firefighter's most useful tools is the infrared camera. This detects sources of heat. It allows a firefighter to see a person's body through thick smoke.

RESCUE!

In July 2010 firefighters were called to a house fire in Blackpool, UK. Two adults and a child were trapped on the roof in dense smoke. Firefighter Dean Seaward scrambled up a ladder to bring the family down. He didn't have any breathing equipment. Afterward he said: "Basically I did my job that every firefighter in the county would do. I don't feel I've done anything special really."

The Great Chicago Fire, 1871

Nobody knows why flames sparked into life in a barn behind DeKoven Street, Chicago, on the evening of October 8, 1871. Fire quickly engulfed the barn. But nobody was too worried. After all, fires were common in the city. But that night a strong wind began to fan the flames toward nearby wooden houses ....

Delayed response

From a tower in central Chicago, fire watchman Mathias Schafer saw a red glow in the southwest. He quickly raised the alarm. But the city's firefighters were slow to respond. Schafer also sent them in the wrong direction. By the time a horse-drawn fire engine finally arrived in DeKoven Street, the fire was out of control.

EYEWITNESS

"A column of flame would shoot up from a burning building, catch the force of the wind, and strike the next one, which in turn would perform the same direful office for its neighbor. It was simply indescribable in its terrible grandeur."

Horace White, editor-in-chief, *Chicago Tribune*

Citizens of Chicago flee over Randolph Street Bridge.

No water

Any hopes of fighting the blaze were dashed when the fire destroyed Chicago's water pumping station. This left the firefighters' hoses dry. Soldiers demolished buildings to make gaps, but sparks simply blew over the gaps.

AT-A-GLANCE

- 200–300 people died
- 90,000 people made homeless
- 17,500 buildings burned down
- 3 sq. mi. (8 sq. km) destroyed
- US$222 million damage

Devastated city

Desperate people escaped by sitting in parks or jumping into the freezing water of Lake Michigan. A third of the city was destroyed before rain helped to stop the fire two days after it started.

The devastated city of Chicago after the fire.

The London Blitz, 1940

German aircraft had dropped bombs on London almost every night in December 1940. But December 29 was different. There were no giant explosions. Instead, Londoners heard gentle thuds as thousands of bombs rained down. These were incendiary bombs—fire starters! The incendiaries burst open, scattering burning liquid that set fire to anything it touched. Some smashed through roofs, spreading fire below.

BREAKING NEWS

December 29, 1940, 6:30 PM, London ...
We are hearing that hundreds of fires are breaking out in the city after a German raid. The whole city seems to be alight. It looks as though the German bombers are trying to destroy St. Paul's. Firefighters are trying to defend the great cathedral.

A German bomber's view of London. Hundreds of these aircraft took part in the raid of December 29, 1940.

The Blitz

The raid was part of a series of attacks known as the Blitz. Thousands of individual fires erupted across the City of London. As the fires took hold, they merged into one. Temperatures soared to more than 1,800°F (1,000°C) Hot air from the fire rose into the air. Fresh air was sucked in to take its place, making the fire even more intense.

Firestorm

A terrifying firestorm raged, carrying flames from building to building, consuming everything in its path. The firestorm was exactly what the Germans wanted. Their plan was to turn London into a pile of rubble, break the morale of Londoners, and force Britain to surrender.

Many Londoners took shelter in the stations of the city's subway system.

EYEWITNESS

"They flashed terrifically, then quickly simmered down to pinpoints of dazzling white, burning ferociously. These white pinpoints would go out one by one, as the unseen heroes of the moment smothered them with sand."

Ernie Pyle, reporter, describing the sight of incendiary bombs falling on London

The London Blitz: Fighting the Fires

The London Fire Brigade was swamped with emergency calls. Fire guards, or "fire spotters," ran through the streets. They tried to put out small fires before they grew too big. Professional firefighters were joined by trained volunteers. Boy scouts guided fire engines through the smoke-filled streets.

AT-A-GLANCE
- 24,000 incendiary bombs fell on the City of London
- 163 people died
- 2.5 sq. km (2.5 sq. km) of the city was destroyed

Stopping the spread

All night the firefighters grappled with hoses as they sprayed water into burning buildings. They couldn't put out the intense firestorms, so they tried to stop them from spreading. Some firefighters were killed as walls, cracked by the intense heat, fell on them.

Firefighters tried to cool buildings with water to stop the flames from spreading.

SAVING ST. PAUL'S

St. Paul's Cathedral is one of London's most famous landmarks. As the incendiary bombs fell on December 29, 1940, the Dean of St. Paul's and a team of fire spotters waited on the roof. They desperately scrambled about smothering small fires. In the streets below, firefighters kept the approaching firestorm at bay. Their tireless efforts saved the great cathedral as fires raged all around.

A famous photograph of the dome of St. Paul's Cathedral standing firm as fires raged around it.

Afterward

Luckily for Londoners, a second wave of bombers turned back because of bad weather. After struggling in the heat all night long, the firefighters finally gained control. People emerged from their underground shelters to find much of their city in ruins. They suffered another five months of bombing before the Blitz finally came to an end.

The Tokyo Firestorm, 1945

It was just after dark on March 9, 1945 when the people of Tokyo heard the drone of aircraft engines overhead. The engines belonged to B-29 Superfortress bombers of the US Air Force. The bomber crews were on a mission to make Japan surrender.

Inferno

Down came the bombs. There was a deadly mixture of fire-starting incendiaries and high explosive bombs. The plan was to create a firestorm that would consume the city. It worked. The incendiaries splashed burning liquid around, setting the wooden buildings of Tokyo on fire. The fires grew into a monstrous inferno that was visible from 120 miles (200 km) away. The firestorm created hurricane-force, super-hot winds that spread the flames.

EYEWITNESS

'Barely a quarter of an hour after the raid started, the fire, whipped by the wind, began to scythe its way through the density of that wooden city.'

Robert Guillain, French reporter

Desperate situation

The people of Tokyo were told to defend their own homes. Many tried with hand water pumps and sand, but the situation was hopeless. Tokyo's firefighters fared no better. With water shortages in the city, their hoses were useless against the giant flames. The police had no time to organize evacuations. Between 80,000 and 200,000 people died in the firestorm.

SAVING LIVES

Firefighters knew they didn't have enough water to tackle the flames. So instead they sprayed the fleeing crowds with water to cool people as they tried to run to safety. Hundreds of people were saved by their actions.

Only stone and concrete buildings survived. Whole blocks of the city simply disappeared in the flames.

Yellowstone Bushfires, 1988

Crash! A bolt of lightning smashes into a tree in Yellowstone National Park. The powerful electric current heats the wood to hundreds of degrees and the wood bursts into flames. In the summer of 1988, this event happened time and again in Yellowstone.

BREAKING NEWS

June 23, 1988, Yellowstone National Park ...

Lightning strikes have set off another fire in Yellowstone today, this time in the Shoshone area. The 1988 fire season is well under way. The park's policy is to let fires burn naturally. So rangers are monitoring the fire, but no attempts are being made to fight it at this time.

Multiple fires

Around 250 fires sparked into life in just three months. Most were caused by lightning. Others were set off by trees falling on electrical power lines. As usual, Yellowstone's rangers allowed the fires to burn naturally. But this time it was a mistake.

Lightning is a common cause of fires in the forests of the United States.

Hot and dry

It had been a dry winter and a hot summer. Grass and pine needles on the forest floor were bone dry. During August, strong winds whipped up the flames. Small fires became large fires, and firestorms were set off. Flames reached 200 feet (60 m) high as trees erupted in fire. Flames jumped roads and firelines. The fires moved through the forest at up to 10 miles (16 km) a day.

Towering flames over Yellowstone in September 1988. The flames leapt over the road soon after.

EYEWITNESS

"As the inferno nears, it roars like a jet engine as the blaze sucks more and more in. You can feel the heat and see the flames half a mile away."

News reporter, the *Billings Gazette*

Yellowstone Bushfires: Fighting Back

For weeks the fires in Yellowstone were allowed to burn. Only in late July did the Yellowstone National Park bosses decide to fight back. More than 9,000 firefighters set off into the forests, supported by dozens of fire trucks, planes, and helicopters. The US Army was called in to help.

Constant battle

Firefighters worked day and night (although the smoke made it hard to know which was which). The forest buzzed with chainsaws as firefighters cleared 800 miles (1,300 km) of firelines. Backfires were lit to burn towards the approaching flames.

These firefighters are hard at work clearing undergrowth to create a fireline to stop the fire from spreading.

Evacuation

The tourist complex around the famous Old Faithful geyser was under threat. Thousands of tourists were evacuated. Firefighters smothered buildings in water and foam to keep them cool.

SAVING THE ENVIRONMENT

Thousands of Yellowstone's trees were saved by dumping fire retardant on them from aircraft. These special chemicals stop trees from bursting into flames so quickly.

ONE YEAR ON

The fires left the forest blackened, with no signs of life. But fire is a natural event in forests, and plants are adapted to survive. Within a year the ground was covered in grass, wildflowers and new saplings.

An airplane releases its load of fire retardant onto burning trees in Yellowstone National Park.

The end

Still the fires burned. The end only came in sight in mid-September, when the fires fizzled out following rain and snow.

AT-A-GLANCE

- No lives lost as a direct result of fire
- 1,235 sq. mi. (3,213 sq. km) of forest damaged, including millions of trees
- 67 buildings lost, costing US$3 million
- 396 elk and other large animals killed

Mont Blanc Tunnel, 1999

Gilbert Degrave jumped from his truck to find smoke pouring from its engine. Flames set light to the truck body, the cargo of margarine and flour inside, and the fuel tank.

Suffocating heat

Degrave's truck was halfway along the Mont Blanc road tunnel, deep under the Alps. Thick, toxic smoke filled the tunnel, forcing other drivers to stop. The fire jumped to their vehicles. The tunnel concentrated the heat, creating temperatures of more than 1,800°F (1,000°C).

Firefighting teams wait at the French entrance to the Mont Blanc Tunnel during the disaster.

BREAKING NEWS

March 24, 1999, 11:15 AM, Mont Blanc Tunnel ...

The Mont Blanc Tunnel has been closed this morning by thick smoke. Firefighting teams have just entered the tunnel. We have no more details yet. The 6.6-mile (11 km) tunnel links Italy and France.

Trapped

Twenty minutes later, firefighting teams arrived at both ends of the tunnel. The French team was trapped by smoke and abandoned vehicles. They took refuge in one of the tunnel's fire shelters and were rescued five hours later. Italian firefighters got within 1,000 feet (300 m) of the fire but were also forced back.

Some survivors were rescued through fresh-air channels under the road deck, but 39 people died in the smoke and heat. It took two days to put out the fire.

RESCUE!

Ten people survived thanks to tunnel security guard Pierlucio Tinazzi. He put on breathing apparatus and rode into the tunnel on his motorcycle. One by one he ferried survivors to safety. He went back in a final time, but his motorcycle became trapped in burning asphalt and he was killed.

The burned and twisted remains of one of the trucks destroyed by the fire. The damage to the tunnel is evidence of the intense heat.

Enschede Fireworks Factory, 2000

It was mid-afternoon on May 13, 2000 when a fire broke out inside the SE Fireworks factory in the town of Enschede in the Netherlands. Nobody knows what sparked the fire. Perhaps it was an electrical fault, or even vandalism. Whatever it was, flames quickly spread toward containers crammed full of fireworks ...

Race against time

Firefighters rushed to the scene. They fought the fire from three sides, desperately trying to stop it from reaching the containers. People gathered in the streets to see what all the fuss was about, but were kept at a safe distance.

BREAKING NEWS

May 13, 2000, 3:30 PM, Enschede ...

Two huge explosions have rocked the town of Enschede. They are believed to have come from a fireworks factory. Eyewitnesses have reported rockets zooming overhead. Firefighters are on the scene.

A frame taken from a video shows the moment a giant fireball erupted over Enschede as flames reached an underground firework bunker.

Big bang

Then disaster struck. Two firework containers exploded, killing four firefighters. A few minutes later, things got even worse. The flames reached 195 tons of fireworks in an underground storage bunker. People living 20 miles (32 km) away heard the bang. Houses around the factory were flattened. The next job for the firefighters and police was to find survivors in the rubble of their homes.

EYEWITNESS

"There was a big explosion and everything was thrown into the air. We were about half a mile away but the house was shaking and there was a mass panic. Fireworks were landing in the streets."

Gordon Coles, resident of Enschede

AT-A-GLANCE

- 23 dead; 950 injured
- 400 houses destroyed
- 1,250 homeless
- US$600 million damage

Remains of buildings and vehicles close to the centre of the explosion at Enschede. Brick walls were knocked down instantly by the main explosion.

Buncefield Fuel Depot, 2005

In the early morning darkness of December 11, 2005, nobody noticed the gasoline pouring down the sides of Storage Tank 912. Engineers at the Buncefield Fuel Depot didn't know the tank was full to the brim. They just kept on pumping fuel in. Gasoline fumes spread silently across the depot ...

Explosion

At 6:01 AM something—possibly a piece of electrical equipment—caused a spark. An explosion ripped through the depot, setting other fuel storage tanks ablaze. People living around the depot woke to find gaping holes in their roofs, walls, and windows.

A plume of toxic black smoke billows up from the roaring flames at the Buncefield Fuel Depot.

Battling the blaze

Buncefield's own firefighting team was first on the scene. Within minutes, two fire trucks arrived. Firefighters searched for missing workers before tackling the fires. By now, 20 fuel tanks were ablaze.

The emergency team grew to 25 fire trucks and 180 firefighters. They sprayed foam over the tanks. Meanwhile, police evacuated 2,000 people from the surrounding area. It took four days to bring the fires under control.

Firefighters fire foam onto the oil tanks to try to smother the flames. Fires still rage in the background.

EYEWITNESS

"It was like something my father described to me during the Blitz, when you could see the whole of London lit up. It was on that sort of scale."

John Bachelor, Fire Service Commander

SAVING THE ENVIRONMENT

Close by the burning fuel tanks were more tanks, also full of aviation and road fuel. Firefighters had to keep these cool. So they created a curtain of water around the burning tanks by spraying water into the air.

Black Saturday Bushfires, 2009

The firefighters of Victoria were expecting trouble on Saturday February 7, 2009. The Australian state was roasting in record temperatures, and the bush was bone dry after a long drought. What actually happened exceeded their worst fears ...

Sparks

Strong southerly winds toppled a faulty power line, and sparks ignited tinder on the ground. Other fires were started by power lines, too, or faulty machinery or cigarettes.

A fire truck near the township of Tonimbuk, Victoria, Australia, with ferocious flames in the background.

AT-A-GLANCE

- 173 dead
- More than 2,000 homes destroyed
- 7,500 people made homeless
- 950,000 acres (350,00 ha) of bush lost

Fatalities

The strong winds spread the fires. A cloud of smoke 9 miles (15 km) high billowed up from the giant Kilmore East firestorm. Some fled as the fires swept toward their towns. Others stayed to defend their homes. Many died in their houses and cars.

Powerless to help

Fires had been forecast. Around 3,500 firefighters were ready, armed with fire trucks, bulldozers, spotter planes, and helicopters. But they couldn't hold back the roaring flames or rescue people.

The firefighters stationed in the small town of Kinglake had gone to defend a nearby town when the flames arrived. The fast-moving and unpredictable fires made it impossible for police to lead people to safety.

SAVING ANIMALS

Volunteer firefighter David Tree discovered a koala with burned paws. The lucky animal was named Sam. He became a symbol of hope for the rescuers. Animal charities took in hundreds of injured animals, including koalas, kangaroos, and wallabies.

Sam the koala takes a drink of water from firefighter David Tree after being rescued from the bushfires.

Learning Lessons

The job of firefighters is not finished when they have put out the flames and packed away their hoses. There's always something to learn from a fire. By sifting carefully through the charred remains, and talking to eyewitnesses, expert firefighters can find plenty of clues. They can often work out where, when, and why a fire started, how it spread and what happened during the fire. These fire investigations may help to prevent fires in the future.

Better and safer

The deadly Mont Blanc Tunnel fire showed that the original fire safety systems were not good enough. For example, there were no sprinkler systems or smoke extractors. The tunnel was rebuilt with these features and safer fire refuges for drivers.

Despite the damage and destruction, firefighters can still find clues to the cause of a fire.

+ SAVING LIVES

A hundred years ago people didn't bother too much about fire safety in buildings. But over the decades fire safety has improved. In most countries today the law insists that public buildings must have smoke detectors, fire alarms, and clearly marked fire escapes.

A simple and inexpensive smoke alarm is a life saver. It gives people a chance of escaping before fire spreads.

Striking early

After the Yellowstone bushfires in 1988, the National Park authorities changed their firefighting plans. They now tackle natural fires before they get too hot to handle.

AT-A-GLANCE

Here are some important fire prevention and safety methods:
- Conduct regular tests of electrical and gas equipment
- Store fuels and inflammable items in safe containers
- Test fire extinguishers, fire alarms, and smoke alarms
- Practice fire drills
- Keep fire escapes clear
- Build with fire-resistant materials

Glossary

backfire A bush or forest fire lit deliberately by firefighters to burn toward an approaching natural fire, designed to burn away fuel so the natural fire is stopped.

Blitz The nightly bombing of London by Germany in 1940 and 1941, during World War II.

chemical reaction When two or more materials combine together and change to make new materials (for example, when methane gas and oxygen react, they make water and carbon dioxide).

drought A long period of time when there is much less rain than normal.

fireline A corridor in a bush or forest made by firefighters by cutting and clearing vegetation, designed to stop fire from spreading.

fire retardant A material that helps to stop materials from burning, or slows down how quickly they burn.

firestorm A huge, very intense fire that sends smoke and hot gases into the air and creates its own gale-force winds that make it even more intense.

fire triangle The three things that are needed for a fire to start—heat, fuel, and air.

fuel Any material that burns in a fire.

fumes Smelly gases created when a liquid such as gasoline evaporates, or gases created during a fire, which can be poisonous.

geyser A place where steam and hot water, heated by hot rocks underground, are blasted into the air.

high explosive An explosive that detonates very suddenly, causing a powerful shockwave.

incendiary bomb A bomb designed to start a fire (rather than to destroy things with a blast).

inflammable Describes a material that catches fire easily.

infrared Invisible rays given off by any warm or hot object.

meteorite A lump of rock from space that hits the Earth.

natural fire A fire that starts naturally—for example, by a lightning strike.

ranger A person who looks after a natural area, such as a forest.

refuge A place of safety.

smoke detector A device that detects tiny amounts of smoke in the air, designed to set off an alarm when a fire has started.

smoke extractor A device that sucks smoke from a building or a tunnel.

spotter plane A plane used by firefighters to see where bush fires are burning, so that firefighters can be sent to the scene.

sprinkler system A system of smoke detectors and water sprinklers, designed to detect and put out fires in buildings automatically.

toxic Describes a material that is poisonous.

water pumping station A building where water is pumped from underground, from a lake or a river, into water supply pipes.

Further Information

Books

The Great Fire by Jim Murphy (Scholastic, 2006)
In Time of Need: Fire by Sean Connolly (Franklin Watts, 2004)
Turbulent Planet: Forest Furnace: Wild Fire by Mary Colson (Raintree, 2004)
Wildfires (Earth in Action) by Matt Doeden (Capstone, 2010)

Web Sites

www.chicagohs.org/fire/intro/wom-index.html
   Chicago fire web of memory

www.museumoflondon.org.uk/archive/exhibits/blitz/index.html
   The Museum of London online exhibition on the Blitz

www.nps.gov/yell/naturescience/wildlandfire.htm
   US National Park Service information about wild fires

www.smokeybear.com/kids/default.asp?js=1
   The US Forest Service's most famous bear gives fire-prevention tips.

www.usfa.dhs.gov/kids/flash.shtm
   US Fire Administration for Kids

Index

Page numbers in **bold** refer to pictures.